HOW TO HAVE
"THE CONVERSATION"

*Talking with Family About
End of Life.*

NORMAN CRAMPTON
and the
REV. DONALD A. JONES

ISBN: 978-1-4834-9450-0 (sc)
ISBN: 978-1-4834-9449-4 (e)

Lulu Publishing Services rev. date: 02/26/2019

HOW THIS BOOK FITS INTO LIFE PLANS

A growing number of older people are beginning to think about having what's called "The Conversation" with family members and close friends—talking about the practical and spiritual matters that become important toward the end of life. And that's new. Death is probably the last taboo topic in America.

But this book is set years before a crisis, when you're blessed with good health, can talk confidently—and expect to live forever!

This book is for caring people. It's practical, readable, and concise, providing both motive and plan for having the conversation with offspring and friends about those things we've all been avoiding. So, have a look inside. You'll even find a chapter on—writing your own obituary!

With all best wishes from the authors.

CONTENTS

CHAPTER 1

Sitting Down for "The Conversation"

- How to approach America's most sensitive topic
- Deciding who, when, and where
- Taking notes
- Reasonable expectations for your first chats
- Dealing with pushback: teachable moments

Do you remember when your parents took you aside for "The Talk"? When they revealed the secrets of the birds and bees? And how you knew all the details already and why were they embarrassing you like that!? When, where, and from whom you learn "The Facts of Life" marks a milestone in just about everyone's life.

By comparison, a sit-down chat with family about "The Facts of Death" may seem not only unnecessary but—frankly, morbid. Talking about death in the first-person may be the only remaining taboo topic in America. Death happens; change the subject.

But that's changing. Talking with loved ones about your eventual death, especially when you're full of life, is slowly becoming the sort of thing a thoughtful person at least begins to consider at some point in a full life. By comparison with the birds and bees, preparing to talk with loved ones about your death takes patience, prayer, determination, tact, and no small amount of courage. That's why this grown-up version of "The Talk" has a grown-up name: "The Conversation."

Raising the Subject

This book responds to your interest in creating some understanding with your family and perhaps also close friends about what you're thinking about death and how they can help you with plans and decisions. Your conversation is more than a thoughtful thing to do. In many ways it's rooted in your faith tradition, and you will see some of those roots in these pages. Full disclosure: the authors are Episcopalians.

Deciding when and where to begin your conversation while you're look-ing and feeling great—in the prime of life—is perhaps the most sensitive matter you've ever faced. But you've given it some thought, and even made some notes. You're ready.

Here are two ways to raise the subject:

- You take the initiative by saying something like, "I wonder if you can help me think about what I'm going to need in terms of health care and—well—everyday life when I'm older and not as fit as I am today. I want to manage things so that I don't become a burden on anyone."
- You listen for an opportunity to begin a conversation when a family member takes the initiative and says, for example, "Mom, have you thought about where you're going to live when staying in the house gets to be too much for you?" And you respond, "I'm so glad you asked!"

When you feel comfortable talking and the moment's right, you gently get to the point: that if you're ever unable to say what you want from loved ones, you'll say it right now. And they don't have to memorize it—you'll send notes! This book will help you with the notes.

You know what will work best, given your personal style and your under-standing of family. If they know you as a well-organized, take-charge type, raising the topic yourself will seem entirely in character, even if privately they say, "Guess what Dad wants to talk about *now*!" That's okay. The point is to get started.

Current topics also can prompt the conversation. Hardly a day passes when health care isn't in the news: Medicare, Medicaid, Obamacare, drug costs, insurance costs, doctors' offices, nursing homes, daughters becoming caregivers to their parents (as they do far more often than sons).

Deciding who's included in the conversation

Who are the people who would be affected at once by a sudden change in your health and living situation—the few people who would help to make decisions about your care? Those are the most important people around the table when you begin to share thoughts and make plans. Often that means your children and your siblings.

Depending on how many miles separate you from immediate family, the key people could be your close, long-time friends. You understand family dynamics and can decide, but the important thing is to let everyone know about your agenda—no secrets—and not to exclude anyone who expresses an interest in helping. Bear in mind there are practical limits to the number of people who can participate productively in a conversation—about any topic.

Deciding when and where you'll talk

Talking face-to-face is the best choice, particularly when you begin the conversation. On the back porch, around the fireplace, at the kitchen table, at a favorite meeting place where you can be close and comfortable. You need to be physically close to the others to hear tones of voice and read faces and use that feedback as a guide going forward. Living nearby makes everything easier—you can take advantage of the right time practically anytime.

If you live far from the younger generation but see them occasionally, making the first conversation part of a regular family gathering may work. But if get-togethers usually coincide with high holidays, talking on those days about your eventual death may not be the best idea. So, pick your gatherings with care. Independence Day may be better than, say, Thanksgiving or Christmas.

"Talking" long distance: Skype, smartphone

Social media have brought us closer to one another in so many good ways. You count on your regular connections with friends and family. But there's a limit to electronics. Call it "bandwidth," which is quite narrow on a smartphone compared to up-close-and-personal. So rather than initiating this conversation on social media, plan to use the phone primarily to follow up and clarify the sit-down, face-to-face exchange.

Deciding how much to say at first

It depends. Even your best-planned and rehearsed words on this subject may be pushed aside when the others hear them for the first time. You're raising one of the most sensitive subjects in American culture, so be patient and keep your sense of humor when others interrupt your sensible, logical, caring-sharing of deeply-felt needs.

Probably the best result of a first conversation is simply the understanding and acceptance by listeners that you want to talk seriously with them about your future. The best takeaway could be simply hearing what family say about their feelings concerning your agenda. Listen carefully and quietly. They're telling you what they need to know to fully, prayerfully join you along the road ahead. The initial conversation is only the beginning. You'll be talking a lot—and that's good.

Taking notes

After a conversation you'll need some notes to remind you about what you shared with loved ones, and what they said in reply. A digital voice recorder—small, unobtrusive—could be useful. Your smartphone may have that capacity. Maybe all you need is paper and ballpoint to jot down a few key items. Or maybe you need—only your keen perception and memory to put it all together in summary form. What's important is to produce soon afterwards a revisable record of the conversation—in a form that you can share online with each person, with a request to give you feedback on what you've noted. You really do want to know whether what you heard reflects what family and close friends believe they said. Don't leave any room for misunderstanding! We'll return to this reminder in later chapters.

Responding when you get pushback

It's normal for family to feel uncomfortable when you—in the full bloom of health and planning a trip to some glamorous place—just casually remark, "Oh, let's sit down sometime soon and talk about my plans for end-of-life."

"Sure, Mom," your daughter laughs—"when you get back from Sun Valley!"

Again, you're raising the last taboo topic in America. And it's common and perfectly understandable, and an expression of love, to hear family and friends object, vigorously, at the mere thought of losing you. Especially among believers, you may hear that "death is in God's hands," and you can agree, adding, "so is life, and that's what we need to share fully."

If pushback sounds like, "Oh, Dad, relax! You know you can count on us to do the right thing," give them a smile and say, "I know you will. But I'll feel a lot better if we can cover a few things." And make plans to do so.

Trouble getting started?

So, you're having trouble getting started. There's a card game that may get you rolling, even if you don't usually play cards. It's called "GoWish" (simple as "Go Fish"). There are two decks of 36 cards and two players. Each card expresses a "wish" that the player may have when facing death, like "To be treated the way I want," "To be free from pain," "To have close friends near," "To meet with clergy or a chaplain." To play the game, you consider the statement on each card and place it on one of three piles labelled "Very important," "Somewhat important," "Not important."

You can see where this is going: two players, two points of view about what's important, an exchange of views. "This can be a good game to play with someone who might become your health-care agent," the instructions say. Another obvious player is a friend or family member with whom you are very close. "GoWish" cards are available from The Coda Alliance, in Silicon Valley.

If talking directly with family is just too much for you to handle right now, you may want to do some background reading-thinking. The "PS" section at the back of this book describes a number of useful references, mostly books.

When non-family learn what you're doing: teachable moments

Once you initiate "The Conversation" and it's going well, you may want to talk about the process with people outside the family circle. Sharing your experience when you meet with friends could interest them in doing the same—or not! You may learn quickly why talking about your eventual death is not what folks talk about much in America. Not while we're having such a good time!

For reflection:

Holy God, you have placed us in family and community. Inspire our consideration of plans for our final days, that we may have a candid, loving conversation with our family or friends.

CHAPTER 2

Warmup Exercise: Writing Your Obituary (For Fun!)

- **Avoiding a dreary first sentence**
- **Writing the key phrase that captures your essence**
- **Naming friends among survivors**
- **Publishing your obit, checking authenticity**
- **Burglar alert!**

It may seem peculiar to write your own obituary, even to noodle around with a few words mostly for amusement. You're perfectly healthy and pass all the Alzheimer's tests (quick—name ten words beginning with Q!). You can imagine what your kids will say when you tell them what you're doing. "You're *what*?!"

So you laugh and say, yes, that sounds a bit odd, but you know how well-organized I am, and I thought it would be fun just to jot down what I'd like people to read about me when I—*ahem*—die. And your son or daughter or sister or brother or other significant other will say, guaranteed, "That's ridiculous—you're going to live forever!"

Of course you are. But isn't it interesting how you always check the obits? People of a certain age always read the obit page. You want to know who's passing away and why, and how old they are, especially how old they are.

And there's nothing morbid about checking the obits. All in good fun. Or as John Cleese of "Monty Python" fame confided recently to an auditorium full of Indiana University undergraduates, "The nice thing about being really old is you're going to be dead soon." (Peals of laughter.)

But more to the point, and looking way down the road, it's simply thoughtful to prepare a rough draft of your obit (and send email copies to family who understand your quirks), saying exactly what you want to say, a statement that only needs to be updated when family learn of your death. Picking up after you, there's so much to do that a head-start on this initial piece of paperwork can be a huge relief at a time when loved ones still can't believe that you're gone.

The important first sentence

If you've spent any time reading obits, you know they follow a pattern. The first sentence always states the full name of the deceased, including nickname, possibly; age at death, residence or place of death, and the date and sometimes the cause of death. (Yes, in this warm-up exercise you'll skip date and cause.)

Often the first sentence also contains an expression added by the survivors like "Surrounded by loved ones" or "Dear spouse for 50 years," phrases that are well meant and can be just as effective in the second or third paragraph.

The best obit is one that captures your being right at the top, in the first sentence. So, in this exercise you'll compose a rather short phrase immediately following your name that says in so many words who you are and how you'd like to be remembered outside the immediate family (who know too much about you already).

Recall the obits you've read in newspapers about the deaths of celebrities or public figures. The first sentence always contains a middle phrase that neatly summarizes who the person was. Here are a few examples about people you probably remember:

"...the wholesome ingénue in 1950s films like 'Singin' in the Rain'..."

"…called himself the greatest and made good the claim…"

"…at 77, became the oldest man in space…"

Of course you know them, and they're identified at the end of this chapter.

If you're a really big deal, *The New York Times* or the *Washington Post* or the *L.A. Times* already have a fairly up-to-date story about you in the files. It's called an "advance," a short biography for use in the event of your demise, lacking only the facts about your finale. Obit writers at the big newspapers occupy spare time keeping these stories fresh, including the key phrase in the first sentence.

Here are two more examples of the key phrase, culled from news coverage:

"…whose accidental discovery of a product called Kitty Litter made cats more welcome household company and created a half-billion-dollar industry…"

"…the irrepressible gas station proprietor and farmer who vaulted to national celebrity in his brother Jimmy's successful campaign…"

The gas station proprietor, you may have guessed, was Billy Carter. Notice how much info has been packed into those phrases. You don't have to write more than a dozen or so well-chosen words to produce your micro-biography. More examples, all from newspaper obits:

"…whose unstinting service to his family, church and community was a hallmark of his life…"

"…brilliant surgeon, civic leader, accomplished athlete…"

"…a well-respected theatrical agent…"

"…talented artist, witty, joyful, loving…"

And this wonderful, seven-word declaration:

"…infinitely generous, invariably opinionated, caring, loyal, brave…".

The additional reason to shape the first sentence of your obit around the key middle phrase is to keep readers reading about you. According to studies, most obit readers, unless they're family, don't read past the first paragraph. So, if the first paragraph is only routine facts, there goes the full story of your life.

Getting started

Humble old you—you may think there's nothing all that special about your life. Beg to differ. You have unique qualities that only begin with "witty, joyful, loving". In this book, everyone merits the full phrase in the first sentence of the obit. Your first step in writing the rough draft is to decide on the key words. If they don't quite arise, ask a friend or family-member, "In just a few words, how would you describe me?" Have some fun with it, but don't say why you're asking—not yet, anyway.

Names of survivors

The longest part of most obits is the list of survivors. You know the immediate family—spouse, children, grandchildren—so beginning the long recitation "He is survived by…" won't be difficult, just essential and often tedious. Listing your brothers and sisters and their families, and perhaps step-siblings and step-parents, will take time.

If you have trouble recalling the names of everyone who really should be acknowledged—nieces and nephews, for instance—a very good resource may be the obituary of another family member who recently died. If you don't have a copy of the obit you may be able to get one from the funeral home that handled arrangements, or from the newspaper where the obit appeared.

Other resources include your greeting-card list, email address list, and the photo from the family reunion you attended recently. And if one of the kinfolk is working on a family tree, she may already have asked for your assistance and is willing to share. The important thing about the survivors' list is just to get started and work on it over time. And as you begin to share your draft obit with family members (won't that be a blast!), you'll surely receive additions and corrections. Remember, it's nothing personal, just all in the family. Even an imperfect list will relieve your survivors of much of the burden at a very difficult time, and they'll say, "Can you believe how thoughtful she was to do all this?"

Names of dear friends

It's not commonly done but entirely proper to recognize the names of people who are not family members but long- time, dear friends. Often, you're as close to friends as to family, and your obit is a proper place to say so. Following the list of family-related survivors you can add something like, "…and also leaves behind long-time friends…", with the names following. But be prepared: you'll probably get some questions from family members who are unacquainted with your personal life, and pushback from others who are well acquainted with your personal life and skeptical about your friendships. That's their problem.

When someone else writes your obit

In the highly organized business of death and disposition in America, someone other than a family member usually writes the obituary from facts provided by the survivors. Most often this means the funeral home staff member who takes down all the family details in a quiet interview. The funeral home or cremation service prepares a routine, humdrum draft and runs it by a family member for approval and arranges for publication.

An obit put together by a well-meaning third-party certainly will omit the phrase in the first sentence that captures the essential you. So, if you're advising survivors to engage the services of an undertaker or cremation service, be very clear that you want your draft-obit used word-for-word.

Details about the funeral

If your religious life has centered for years on one parish and the church office has your instructions concerning your funeral service—well done!

Noting the place in this early draft obit will connect survivors with the location and, perhaps, the details you've already decided on—Chapter 6 of this book concerns those details. If you already have a burial site or a columbarium niche, for example, or if a graveside service is planned, those decisions can go in the draft.

Will you say something about flowers? They're beautiful gifts to survivors. But the sudden arrival of lots of flowers also is a big management problem. For family, the questions are where do the flowers go and how will they be kept fresh? And where should the flowers go after services? So it's helpful in your instructions to family to name a florist and make arrangements to have flowers delivered and properly placed. If you're planning to meet with church staff to get your wishes on file, plans for flowers often are part of discussion. Funeral homes routinely manage flower logistics.

If instead of flowers you prefer memorial gifts to a favorite charity, provide the name and full address of where the gift should be sent. But do think about family politics: your favorite charity or social cause may raise a red flag with kin.

There's also a place in your instructions to survivors about how you'd like to be recognized at a wake or in a eulogy at a religious service. Again, the tone is in the first sentence.

Beware: Burglars read obits

This caution leaps far ahead, but it's worth noting now. Burglars, like the rest of us, look for opportunity. Some enterprising burglars check the obit pages for houses that may be empty a few hours during your funeral. Even if your address does not appear in your obit, it's easy to find with a Google search. So, advise your loved ones to appoint someone to stay behind and guard your place when everyone else is at the service. And think about how you'll keep your place secure when the mourners have gone home. Make sure your mail and newspapers don't pile up out front; use timer switches to turn lights on and off; and if there's a vehicle parked in the driveway, arrange to have it jockeyed around so it doesn't look abandoned. There's more about this in Chapter 7.

Other things to say in the obituary

After the list of survivors you can expand upon the key phrase in the first sentence of the obit with details about what you did in the prime of life (and may still be doing), such as military service, employment, hobbies, and honors. Among the many advantages to writing your own obit, you decide how much to say about your illustrious life, leaving nothing to the well-meaning but fallible humans who survive.

But you don't have to write a lot. Here are two good examples:

"...loved bridge, euchre, Notre Dame, martinis, Coca-Cola, Frosted Flakes, Scrabble, but most of all her family and friends."

"...enjoyed gardening, hummingbird watching, cooking, sewing, traveling to Florida..."

Getting your obit into print

In your instructions, give the name of the newspaper where you'd like your obituary to appear and the names and addresses of alumni and professional magazines, fraternal orders, etc., that can receive email copies of the obit.

Newspapers charge to print obits. The longer the obit (measured in typeset lines or column inches), the greater the charge. There are exceptions. In smaller communities, a short notice containing only the bare essentials— name, address, date and place of death, age—may be accepted at no charge as a news item. That's the case at the Bloomington, Indiana, *Herald-Times,* for example. But if you'd like your Bloomington neighbors to know the whole story with lots of biographical information, you'll pay about $180 for about 350 words, including a photo, according to the newspaper.

And that's a bargain. If you want your obit to run in *The New York Times,* there's a 4-line minimum (counting 26 characters per line) for $263. That's the lowest cost. Each additional line costs $53, according to the classified advertising department. Thus, the Bloomington, Indiana, obit of 350 words running one day in the *Times* would cost close to $3,500. Photo extra.

Speaking of photos, think about how you'd like to look in that obit photo, and be honest. You looked terrific in the college yearbook, but you've added lots of character in your face since then, and it shows in a good contemporary shot. Ask your grandchildren to pick their favorite photo of you.

How the publication checks for authenticity

Newspapers are very careful to check the authenticity of obits and death notices. They don't want to become accomplices in a practical joke announcing your bogus departure—and leading to an enormous lawsuit brought by you when you quit laughing.

Because most obits are submitted for publication by funeral directors or cremation service companies, the newspaper will verify authenticity with a phone call back to the service provider. If, on the other hand, you and your survivors want direct burial on your property (where doing so is permitted by state and local regulations) you must provide proof of your death if you intend to have a death notice published somewhere. That means your survivors will need to produce a death certificate (see Chapter 5).

To close this chapter, the three obit phrases cited earlier belong to Debbie Reynolds, Muhammad Ali, and John Glenn.

For reflection:

Holy God, you have shared deeply in my life story. Guide my recollections that I may prepare an obituary which will inspire others in their life stories.

CHAPTER 3

Accidents, Unexpected Illnesses

- **Finding you fast!**
- **Strategies for home, work, abroad**
- **Living Will, Advance Directive, health-care representative**
- **DNR—Do Not Resuscitate**
- **Placing your documents where they'll be found (you hope!)**

This is about the phone call that family receive when you've suffered misfortune and need help. Who knows where you'll be—at home and taken a fall? In a clinic off the Champs Elysees? On a boat, circling Manhattan?

The purpose of this chapter is to help you prepare family to find you and, even though they may be far away, help you to be treated the way you want to be by emergency responders. There's nothing magical about any of this—it's all about taking certain steps and sharing the essential information with the people who need to know.

The hospital you're likely to be taken to

After we "settle down" in life, which may mean moving to a warm place, for example, or into a condo in a northern city, most of us spend most of our days in the same neighborhood, give-or-take a few miles for regular things like volunteer work or doctor visits or distant shopping.

If you've lived in the same place for some years, you may have made a number of visits to the same nearby hospital. If you've had the same address forever, your children may have been born in that hospital. And if you should wind up there because of accident or serious illness, your family, when they get the call, at least can picture the place, and that knowledge can offer a bit of reassurance. Double-check your website to make sure info for the hospital is up to date.

"In case of accident…"

You probably carry in your wallet a card with the inscription "In case of accident…" and you've written a phone number there of the person to be notified. Today, before going any further, check that number to make sure it's current. As you know, landline telephones are disappearing as people adopt smartphones as their way to connect with the rest of the world. The phone number you wrote after "In case of accident…" may no longer be in service.

Another way to "carry ID" is to put it on your shoes, probably the pair you wear most while out and about. The company RoadID in Fort Mitchell, Kentucky, sells a stainless steel tag to attach to shoelaces. It's engraved with your name and the names and phone numbers of your important contacts.

The home scene

Home alone, your biggest risk is that something happens, you need help, and no one's there to come to your aid. Perhaps—careful planner that you are—you're wearing a help-button necklace and an operator is standing by 24-7. Or you're talking on your smartphone when calamity arrives and you still have a grip on the phone, and the person at the other end has the presence of mind to call 911 for you—if you're unable to dial it yourself.

But if calling 911 won't work because the person you're speaking with lives in another community—or another state, or overseas—it's far better for that person to call the local number you've given her for such emergencies. Possibly the best number is the police department serving your area.

On vacation

Check the statistics—not very many people die on vacation. That's why the insurance company that sells you the just-in-case policy to whisk you back home in the event of illness pays such nice dividends to its shareholders. You're a pretty good risk, so relax and enjoy.

But in the extremely rare event that you suffer an accident or illness while far from home, it's important that the careful preparations you've made at home have followed you. Will they? If you're traveling with people who are empowered to make decisions on your behalf (see "Advance Directive," following), you're in good hands. If not, or if you're traveling alone, the "In case of accident" info becomes vital, so, again, make sure it's current.

At work

Some people say the best place to suffer sudden illness or accident is your workplace, and the authors agree. You'll probably be within sight of other workers, who can rush to your aid. If you need transport to a hospital it will be at company expense (yes!). There will be no questions about your identity or the person to call in this emergency because your employer has that info in the company system and can pull it up at once. Co-workers can take care of your personal belongings. All things considered, the workplace is a pretty good place to be when you need help in a hurry. So, keep working!

Of course, your "workplace" also can be the place where you volunteer all those hours every week (doing church work, for example). Or it can be the place where you go regularly for R&R to give your housemate some relief from your amusing presence. Just be sure to have ID in a pocket.

Empowering your decisions: Living Will,
Advance Directive

The following section is about the paperwork that empowers your decisions about your health care in an emergency situation. To begin, it's important to distinguish between the Will that you prepared some years ago (you

17

did, didn't you?) and a Living Will. What you have said in your Will only takes effect after you're dead. While you're alive, what you need for some assurance that your careful instructions about end of life will be carried out is a Living Will, which is very much like an Advance Directive.

But first, about that Will you never prepared. You stand shamed with the majority of Americans. A Gallup poll in 2016 found that only 44 percent of the U.S. population have a will. However, among the 65-and-older group, 68 percent do have a will, so if you're in the minority of your age group, talk to a lawyer about drawing up a will.

Living Will

Your Living Will expresses your decision, to quote from one such document, "that my dying shall not be artificially prolonged" under the circumstances you then describe, including incurable injury, disease, illness, or permanent unconscious state. You let all the important people know that you have prepared a Living Will, beginning with your physician, who will keep a copy in your file. And your doctor's file should be readily accessible, preferably online, so that your decisions can be immediately known wherever you are being treated. But note that "wherever" is global and challenging under the best circumstances. You can reasonably expect that your Living Will will be observed in home territory—your physician has it, your hospital has it in your records, you've stowed it visibly in the freezer at home. Farther afield, your sharing of your Living Will with family and close friends—possibly shared with them online—is as close as you can get to a guarantee that it will be observed.

Advance Directive

"Advance Directive" is a broad term that includes among other things the powers of Living Will and Appointment of a Health Care Agent (or Advocate). But the exact definitions of all those terms, and the forms you'll prepare to put them into force, all are determined by your state of residence. So, a good place to begin is to go online and search the term "Advance Directive" followed by the name of your state. That should lead you to complete materials, including forms. Another good source is www.

caringinfo.org, a nonprofit in Alexandria, Virginia, that can deliver the essentials for your state. The following is general guidance only and not a substitute for legal advice.

An Advance Directive for health care is a form that you prepare to state your preferences for health care in the event you lose the ability to make decisions yourself. If the form is properly prepared and if it is available when needed, an Advance Directive protects your right to refuse medical treatments you don't want or request treatments you do want.

To illustrate, an Advance Medical Directive may be a check-off form where you can choose "I want" or "I do not want," for example, CPR, breathing machine, kidney dialysis, major surgery, blood transfusions.

Suppose you need surgery for something familiar, like gallstones. If you're in pretty good shape as a 65-year-old, your doctor could advise an out-patient procedure, with confidence you'd come through with minimal after-effects.

But suppose you're 85 years old and frail, meaning you've become slow, weak, fatigued, and you've lost weight. Removing those gallstones now means a hospital stay, and the prognosis may not be very good. The risk of dying may be significant; the prospect of diminished functional ability quite real.

What do you decide to say in your Advance Directive about a situation like that? The sentence could begin something like, "If I am frail and at high risk of serious and long-lasting complications..." and continue with your declarations concerning that eventuality.

Note that if you spend time in more than one state, such as Wisconsin in summer and Florida in winter, the prudent course will be to prepare an Advance Directive for each state (yes, the paperwork never ends). And while we're talking about contingencies, note that an Advance Directive may have no effect at all in the event of a medical emergency.

For example, you're driving from Wisconsin to Florida and crash the car somewhere on the way. The emergency medical technicians who speed to the scene are absolutely required to perform CPR (cardiopulmonary resuscitation) if they find you without pulse or not breathing—unless they become immediately aware of a separate order not to perform CPR. Think about where such an order is going to come from on a moment's notice at a crash site. There's more about this at the section below on DNR, Do Not Resuscitate.

Putting aside bad luck, preparing an Advance Directive is a very good idea. And it's rather routine, as you'll see in the form you download for your state. There are three main parts:

1. Appointing a health-care representative
2. Declaring what health-care you want or don't want when you can no longer make those decisions for yourself
3. Getting signatures and witnesses to make the directive legal.

Appointing a health-care representative

States have several titles besides "health-care representative" for this person—health care proxy, durable power of attorney for health care, health care surrogate—and they all define the same role. You appoint this person to make decisions about your medical care if you're unable to make decisions yourself. Anyone 18 years old or older can serve as your rep. Commonly, it's a family member or close friend whom you trust and who clearly understands your wishes and will accept responsibility of making medical decisions for you. You can also appoint a second person to step in if the first person you name is unable to act for you when needed.

When you think about asking a person to speak on your behalf concerning your health and the overall goals of your care, take some time. The first person who comes to mind may, indeed, be your best choice. And it may, indeed, be a member of immediate family or a close friend. But it could be someone else. Your advocate should know you so well that you are confident she or he will make the decisions about your care that you would make if you were able. And you are confident that this person will represent you clearly and strongly when others disagree, as well they may.

Equally important, your health-care representative should be on the scene, nearby. If the hospital is in Connecticut and your representative is in California, imagine the complications of confirming the identity of your advocate and connecting him or her with health-care providers.

The procedure for appointing a health-care representative varies state-by-state. Once again, you can find the instructions for your state at the website caringinfo.org. And, of course, once you have appointed a health-care representative you'll want to let family and close friends know who this person is and how to reach him or her. Better still, before you make the appointment, talk about this decision with family and close friends. It's an important topic for your continuing conversation.

Don't forget dementia

Decisions about providing you with proper care become quite special when you're dealing with dementia at the end of life. One useful resource available online comes from End of Life Choices New York, at endoflifechoicesny.org. Scroll down to "Featured Documents" and you'll find "New Directive: Dementia," covering options for care if you're unable to feed yourself or make informed decisions. You and your health-care rep should discuss.

It never hurts…

Should you suffer a personal injury, family may want to engage a law firm to pursue a personal injury claim, so if you have a particular firm in mind be sure to include the name of the firm in your conversation.

"Code Blue!" and other colors

Just about everyone knows that "Code Blue!" means get out of the way as doctors, nurses, and the rest of the "Code Team" rush to revive a person who has stopped breathing or has no pulse, or both. TV shows in hospital settings also rely on these command performances to keep the story moving. Perhaps surprising, "Code" announcements apparently have no official position in health care—each hospital or clinic can decide how to identify emergencies. Some places say "Code Red!"

The important thing to note for future reference is that a "Code" call almost always means that CPR—cardiopulmonary resuscitation—will applied, so a little history of CPR is in order. It's been practiced on the medical scene since the early 1960s. The idea is to restore breathing and pulse to a victim who has lost both. And if you were a fan of certain TV shows back then, CPR seemed miraculously effective. On "ER" and "Chicago Hope" and "Rescue 911," two-thirds of the victims who had undergone CPR walked away from the hospital functioning fully.

Medical history tells a different story, however. A 2012 study found that only 2 percent of adults who collapsed on the street recovered fully. Among seniors who received CPR in a hospital, 18 percent survived to be discharged. Among patients who received bystander CPR in some non-hospital setting, like workplace or aboard public transit, 16 percent were eventually discharged from the hospital.

So, if you've decided that, for reasons you've thought through clearly and discussed with your physician and family, you do not want CPR, you must be certain this decision is known to everyone, beginning with the people who surround you in an emergency. One step is to adopt DNR.

DNR—Do Not Resuscitate

The abbreviation "DNR" is widely known as shorthand for "Do Not Resuscitate." It is your instruction to emergency health care providers, including EMTs and "Code Blue" teams, not to initiate CPR if you are found not breathing and without a heartbeat. Less widely known, however, is how a person can decide to adopt DNR as his or her decision with some assurance that it will be recognized and complied with in the turmoil of an emergency health setting.

DNR rules differ state to state. In Wisconsin, for example, a person who wants to wear a DNR bracelet to call attention to his or her decision must complete a DNR form requiring an attending physician's name and signature. The form is kept on file at the state and it can be revoked at any time by the person who initiates it.

A valid Wisconsin DNR bracelet displays the internationally recognized symbol "Staff of Aesculapius" and the words "Wisconsin Do-Not-Resuscitate-EMS" and the patient's first and last name on the back.

An emergency provider who sees and complies with such a DNR order will not, quoting the Wisconsin form, "perform chest compressions, insert advanced airways, administer cardiac resuscitation drugs, provide ventilator assistance, or defibrillate." But that does not mean the EMT will ignore keeping the patient as comfortable as possible under the circumstances, by clearing the airway, administering oxygen, positioning the patient for comfort, controlling bleeding, providing pain medication, and providing emotional support.

POLST

POLST is the acronym for "Physician Orders for Life Sustaining Treatment." It's related to DNR but will come into play in different situations. You may think about adopting DNR while you're healthy and fit, as instructions to EMTs, should you suffer an accident, let's say, and are found without pulse and not breathing. Like DNR, POLST is a legal document that's filled out with your doctor and based on your end-of-life decisions.

But POLST comes into play more often with people who are suffering an advanced progressive or terminal illness. A POLST describes the type of care you want in such a situation, and it overrides any procedures that are legally required of emergency personnel.

Enacting a POLST for yourself is regulated by the laws of your state; depending on your state it may have a different name. Here are the other names:

MOST (Medical Orders for Scope of Treatment)

MOLST (Medical Orders for Life Sustaining Treatment)

POST (Physician Orders for Scope of Treatment)

TPOPP (Transportable Physician Orders for Patient Preferences)

Placing your documents so they'll be found when needed

There's a good bit of paperwork related to the steps described in this chapter, and if there's any question about applying your instructions concerning health care, the supporting documents should be readily available in at least three places:

1. Your home, in a widely understood place. That place may be inside the freezer, meaning the large freezer that's separate from the refrigerator. One author also keeps a black, 3-ring binder on his desk labelled "Big Black Book," containing all the originals of documents, indexed. Family members who live elsewhere know where it is.
2. With your doctor in your files at the doctor's office.
3. At the hospital you're likely to be taken to when you're in home territory.

The additional place is the email you've sent to family and friends marked "Save" because it contains these important instructions concerning your health care.

For reflection:

O God, our heavenly Father, whose glory fills the whole creation and whose presence we find wherever we go, surround (me, us) with your loving care, protect (me, us); from every danger, and bring (me, us) in safety to (my, our) journey's end.

CHAPTER 4

Where and How You'd Like to Live Your Whole Life

- **Surviving as an "Elder Orphan"**
- **Home-based care, nursing-home care, assisted living**
- **Thinking about "the right to die"**
- **Distracting the Grim Reaper**

Living all your days in the place you love—home sweet home, that dependable, comforting space, today and tomorrow and ever—who can ask for anything more?

But life keeps happening (*Proverbs, 19:* "Man proposes, God disposes"). Partners die, friends move away, you take a tumble and realize that home sweet home may not be a reliable place anymore. You may need to trade-in your cozy old setting for another offering assurance of more good days living as independently as possible.

Growing numbers of older people live alone, and they've been given a simply awful name: "Elder Orphans." Straight out of Dickens! The term means you're aging without a family caregiver. Your kids live too far away, your close friends and siblings have problems of their own. But you're going to figure it out!

Mark this down as a topic next time you talk with family: where you expect to continue living. For the agenda:

- All things considered, can you remain in the place where you now live? Is it a safe place, meaning the physical layout as well as the neighborhood? How fit are you, physically and mentally? If you need occasional support from non-family, who are those people?
- How much extra care will you need to go about everyday life? Totally independent? Great! But note that according to federal health data, the odds are better than fifty percent you'll need extended care of one kind or another before you die.
- How many assisted-living establishments are there on the local scene? Whom do you know who lives in one, and what do they report? Have you accepted one of those frequent invitations for a free dinner to get acquainted? Yes, do RSVP, no obligation! Moving into assisted living in the community where you've lived a long time can help preserve your long-time friendships.
- How do family feel about your situation? What's important to them? Do they understand and lovingly accept your decision to stay where you are, given the plans you present to them?

Sometimes, family invite the older generation to come live with them, adding a wing on the house and calling it "The Gramatory". Some municipalities are changing zoning laws to permit portable mini-houses to be parked behind the house out front. Wherever you live, you'll probably need at some future time a reliable, ever-ready caregiver to help you with everyday things, like driving you to and from a doctor visit. Think about who that person is.

But more than clinical stuff, there's your need for companionship, conversation, TLC, spur-of-the-moment little adventures to add spark to your days. That's where you really want to live.

Meanwhile: Medicare, Medicaid, etc.

Yes, you know the difference between Medicare and Medicaid, but just to refresh: Everyone who receives Social Security also is eligible irrespective of income for coverage by Medicare. You pay for this healthcare insurance (Medicare Part B) through a monthly deduction from your Social Security check. Medicare is with you for life, covering a large portion of your medical and hospital expenses.

But Medicare doesn't cover all costs for the kind of care you may need as you grow older: home-based care and nursing home care. What are the odds you'll need that sort of care? The Kaiser Family Foundation has reported that one in three people turning 65 will require nursing home care at some point; and the average yearly cost of that care in 2016 was $82,000, "…nearly three times the annual income of most seniors," Kaiser said. A 2015 survey by the Urban Institute and the federal Department of Health and Human Services reported that 52 percent of people reaching age 65 will need this kind of care at some point before they die. Life expectancy and the extent of required care are huge variables, but the survey predicted that about 9 percent of people would spend more than $250,000. The remaining 91 percent would spend somewhat less, still big numbers.

Given these grim statistics, what's important for you to discuss with family? A good place to start may be your net worth, meaning the cash value of everything you own, like real estate, investments, cars, boats, the cash value of life insurance, etc.; minus everything you owe, such as mortgages and other monthly payments, the balance on your home-equity line of credit, balances on your charge cards, contributions (like your church pledge) that remain to be paid.

You probably have a pretty good idea of your net worth without doing a lot of paperwork, and your family possibly do, too. The question for discussion is how long you can expect to pay out of your own assets for the health care you may need in the future. Even if you can't attach exact numbers now, talking it over is useful.

Medicaid is designed for people with few assets and limited income, which surprisingly includes people who have been both successful and thrifty throughout their lives and socked away seemingly plenty of money to cover unexpected things like nursing home care for five-plus years at $82,000 a year. Sometimes, when confronting numbers like those, Medicaid looks like it could be a backstop at some point. But Medicaid places a tight limit on assets, and monthly income including Social Security cannot exceed a few thousand dollars. Note that any planning should be informed by a lawyer who knows exactly how your state runs its Medicaid program.

A useful resource concerning the cost of long-term care and your alternatives for covering the cost is a website prepared by the U.S. Department of Health and Human Services, *longtermcare.gov.*

Thoughts about "the right to die"

Enacted into law in Oregon, Vermont, Washington, New Mexico, Montana, and California, "the right to die" makes it legal for a medical doctor to provide medical aid in dying upon request from a patient who is lucid and has a terminal illness and less than six months to live. The other name for this procedure is "physician-assisted suicide."

Your church connection is relevant here. Consider the findings of a Pew Research Center survey in 2013 of 16 major religious groups about their position on physician-assisted suicide, among other end-of-life questions. Eleven of the denominations reported they did not accept a right to die. They are: Assemblies of God, Buddhism, Catholicism, Church of Jesus Christ of Latter-Day Saints, Episcopal Church, Evangelical Lutheran Church in America, Islam, Judaism, Seventh-Day Adventist Church, Southern Baptist Convention, United Methodist Church.

The spokesperson for Hinduism expressed a general concern about the negative effect on karma from prematurely ending a person's life, while noting that some Hindus believe there are circumstances that justify the hastening of death. The National Baptist Convention reported no specific church teaching on the topic but broad agreement that "one's life is the providence of God, and you let it take its course". Presbyterian Church USA said it had not taken a position.

The United Church of Christ said it supported the right of terminally ill persons to make their own decisions about when to die. Unitarian

Universalist Association said it advocated "the right to self-determination in dying."

A very small proportion of deaths are attributed to physician-assistance, according to government statistics. For example, in 2016 the number of deaths under the Oregon Death With Dignity Act was 37.2 per 10,000 total deaths. Median age of the Oregon patient was 73, and 79 percent were suffering cancer. In Canada, where all provinces have legalized medical assistance in dying, the number of such deaths between January 1 and June 30, 2017, was 1,179, or 0.9 percent of all deaths during that period.

All denominations in the Pew survey reported general support for decisions by a terminally ill person, or his advocate, not to employ "extraordinary means and technologies to delay dying." And Pope Francis agrees. Recently he told participants in a medical conference at the Vatican that stopping treatment for terminally ill people "acknowledges the limitations of our mortality, once it becomes clear that opposition to it is futile."

Living your last days in hospice

Heather Lende, writing in *The New York Times Book Review:* "Hospice care is rooted in the belief that death is a natural part of life, that dying can be managed so that people may remain alert and as pain-free as possible until the end, and that a good death is as much a spiritual experience as it is a physical one, for all involved."

From a brochure distributed in Oregon: "Hospice is a philosophy of neither shortening nor prolonging life but rather letting the terminal illness take its course with care and comfort of symptoms to provide the goal of a peaceful death with dignity."

Admission to hospice, which is supported by Medicare, is simple and direct. A hospice doctor or your regular doctor or nurse practitioner certifies that you're terminally ill and have 6 months or less to live. Hospice care can be provided in the comfort of your home, if that's what you prefer, or in a hospice clinic. The objective in either place is to relieve your physical suffering and provide comfort so that you can be with loved ones until the end. Hospice has become what many regard as the most successful segment of the American health-care industry.

For details about hospice care, you can download the 2016 edition of "Facts and Figures: Hospice Care in America" at the website of the National Hospice and Palliative Care Organization.

Palliative care medicine

Palliative care is related to hospice care in that the primary goal is relief of pain and suffering. But palliative care typically begins at an earlier time, when you're dealing with serious illness, perhaps in hospital, and confronting the side-effects of both disease and treatment. Again, like hospice care, palliative care responds to your emotional, social, and spiritual needs, aimed at an improved quality of life.

Concerning music at bedside

This should be easy: music you'd like to hear when you're *in extremis*. If that seems irreverent, let's hear from the Benedictine monks at Cluny Abbey in France (circa 10th Century) who developed a playlist of Gregorian chants for the dying that could last as long the dying did, or so it has been reported. If your next family roundtable includes grandchildren, they'll surely understand how music speaks to the soul and, while they may not understand your musical tastes, can advise how to put Bach's *B-Minor Mass* on a smartphone right next to your ear.

Better yet, a live performance. A friend with a guitar? Another with a voice? As one observer has put it, "When it comes to the solemnity of the deathbed, live music is already part of the larger movement to reintegrate death into the American culture."

Death defying?

To confirm what you've suspected pages ago, a motive of this book probably is to distract the Grim Reaper. It's the nature of planners to try to avoid surprises, gaining some control over the future. Writing your own obit (Chapter 2) is a good example, and if you've made those words easily available to family they may in fact be exactly what people read about you one day.

For reflection:

O God, our heavenly Father whose glory fills the whole creation and whose presence we find wherever we go, surround (me, us) with your loving care, protect (me, us); from every danger, and bring (me, us) in safety to (my, our) journey's end.

[Adapted from page 831 of *The Book of Common Prayer.*]

CHAPTER 5

Thinking About Family
on the Day You Die

- **Spreading the news**
- **Preparing death certificates**
- **"Green" burial, home burial**
- **Donating your body to science— and your organs to save a life**
- **Perspectives on cremation**
- **Life everlasting on Facebook**

What can you say or do while you're brimming with life to prepare family and friends for the day of your death?

So many times and in so many ways you've said, and they know, that you cherish them. You've tried to reassure them, best you can, that you know your spirit will always live in their hearts, and that you and they will never be separated from the love of God.

The conversations you've had with loved ones over the years perhaps can express, however imperfectly, your care for their feelings. Your plans for this day is a kindness.

The first people likely to know of your death

If you live some distance from family, perhaps you should ask regular companions, if they're the first to know of your death, if they will be your messenger and immediately contact the people who need to know, by telephone. And let family and other close friends know who these people are. Share phone numbers.

If you should die in hospital or hospice, notification of family generally is immediate by telephone because you've provided the contact information upon admittance. First calls also go to your priest and perhaps to a funeral home or burial society or cremation society if you've made those plans.

If your death is by accident, the emergency responders will look for the ID you carry such as a driver license or a card in your wallet inscribed "In case of accident, please call..." Think about the phone number on that card: Is it current, and does it belong to the person who is the most important person to learn of your death at the earliest possible time?

The best way to spread the news

A phone call is the only way for family and close friends to learn of your death. Only the human voice conveys the feelings of this sad news, and the only way to share feelings is a conversation, difficult as it will be. If the other person doesn't answer the phone but asks for a message to be left, the caller should confine the message only to a request to return the call as soon as possible. Email and texting also can be used to ask the recipient to call ASAP, without other details.

Posting on social media

Somewhere on social media is this very good advice—that no one should first learn on social media of the death of a close family member or friend. Every person deserves to hear the news directly from a surviving family member or close friend, not from an online post. In the turmoil of a death and the speed of communication these days, waiting at least 24 hours before posting seems reasonable. That doesn't mean an arbitrary delay will be observed, but it's a guidepost. Talk it over with family and friends.

Arrangements already in place: Church Office

The authors of this book have on file at our church a simple form titled "Requests at the Time of My Death." It contains our instructions concerning the arrangements—whom we'd like to be in charge, disposition of the body, the burial service, requested hymns, etc. We recommend that everyone with a church connection get these kinds of instructions in place. Quoting the document from our church, "This is not a morbid affair but rather an admission of our own mortality and an expression of our care and concern for those we love."

The backup step, as this book recommends, is to prepare an online file with the same details that is shared with family and friends.

Getting all those death certificates (not your job)

When you die, your death must be registered within a few days with the local and state vital-records office. The death certificate usually is prepared by the organization or person with custody of the body. That may mean a funeral home, a cremation service, a green burial society, or even a member of the family in the case of home burial. The certificate requires the signature of a doctor or a medical examiner or a coroner.

As noted earlier, death is wrapped in paperwork, and the death certificate is the first example. The person you have appointed to manage your affairs—perhaps a family member or a close friend—will need a small number of death certificates, and each one must be certified with an official stamp from the public agency that records the death. Photocopies generally are not acceptable at the various places that the survivors need to visit after your death, such as:

--Life insurance, one certificate for each company

--Attorney settling estate issues

--Probate attorney, possibly several certified certificates needed

--Banks, one for each bank and each bank that holds CDs. If asked, a bank generally will make a copy of the certificate and return the original. That's a saving.

--Stocks, one for each company held or for each broker.

--Bonds, one copy for each company bond, one for all U.S. Savings Bonds.

--Bureau of Motor Vehicles, one certificate to transfer title to any vehicle and to cancel your driver license.

--Employer, a copy to redeem all benefits due, including current pay and vacation pay.

--IRAs, 401K/403B/Retirement plans, pensions—one copy for each.

--Health insurance, if the policy contains life insurance.

--Income tax, one copy for each county, state, and federal filing.

--Real estate tax, one copy for each county where you own property.

That's a long list! The good news is that funeral homes and burial societies generally include procuring death certificates as part of their services. Your survivors pay for each certified copy, in the range of $10 to $15 each, and ordering 10 initially is common, based on all the places where a death certificate will be required. The person who has accepted the role of your administrator should be reimbursed this cost from the proceeds of your estate.

Veterans' benefits

Military service veterans are entitled to one "Government Use" death certificate at no charge that your survivors can use, for example, to request an American flag to be presented to survivors at a service, military funeral honors, headstones. Funeral homes usually include procuring this certificate as part of their services. But your survivors can also download the essential forms online at the website vba.va.gov/survivors, or call the local VA office. A veteran also is entitled to burial in a National Cemetery, and if the veteran is married, his or her spouse is entitled to burial next to the veteran. For details and costs, visit the online site just noted.

Your final Social Security check

The Social Security Administration makes a one-time death payment of $255 to your surviving spouse or child. Typically, payment by SSA is initiated by your local health department when the death certificate is being processed. Perchance your regular monthly Social Security payment arrived in your account after your death, a survivor should call the local SSA office to inquire about proper handling of the payment.

"Green" burial, home burial

Before the modern era of funeral homes and cremation services, preparing a body for final disposition usually happened at home—the washing, the dressing or wrapping, the funeral service perhaps at graveside, and the lowering into the earth without a coffin or any other barriers to delay returning the body to earth, dust to dust. This procedure is now called "Green" burial because it's environmentally friendly—no chemicals for embalming, no need for wood, steel, or concrete to place between the body and the earth.

Home burial also can mean burial on property that you own. To be buried on your own land, your survivors probably will need a permit from local government and will have to follow local regulations concerning the site and depth of the grave and perhaps other matters.

If you've talked over home burial or green burial with family members and, though they love you dearly they'd rather not be so hands-on, your local funeral home perhaps will perform all the home procedures including transport of the body to the gravesite. For what's available state-by-state, the website of The Green Burial Society is useful. And if this entire topic seems simply bizarre to family and friends, just smile and remind them that, deep down, you've always been an environmentalist.

Donation of your body to a nearby school of medicine

The option of turning over the whole body to a university department of anatomy to help train physicians and conduct research is rather appealing to some people. You contribute yourself, literally, to the furtherance of science. And it's generally easy to put this option into play. You register your decision with the university and let it be known to all concerned, meaning your family and physician, among others. For the survivors there's no hassle or the expense of funeral home services.

Typically, when the medical school is finished with a corpse, it is cremated and the ashes are returned to the family.

It's been estimated that 17,500 bodies find their way to medical research every year in the U.S. What's unknowable is how many people planned to donate compared to the number of bodies delivered to medical schools. It's easy to register for donation, but future circumstances may prevent donation. Consider the perfect case: the medical school is fairly near the place where you die, and your body is fairly intact when you die. No organ donations have been made except perhaps the eyes. There's been no autopsy. No embalming. An arrangement is in place to transport your body immediately to the medical school morgue upon your death.

Also, you're the right size—not too tall or too heavy. Obesity is a barrier. Medical schools want corpses that are easy to transfer on and off a gurney, and with proportions that facilitate the examination of organs. All things considered, acceptance of your body by a school of medicine may not work. Best to have a Plan B.

Donation of organs

Plan B could be your decision to donate your organs, not the whole body. For detailed information about donation, go to organdonor.gov.

Registering as an organ donor can be done easily online, and many states also allow your donor status to be shown on your driver license.

Cremation and ashes

Within a rather short time, cremation of the body has overtaken ground burial as the preferred method of disposing of remains. According to the National Funeral Directors Association, in 2016 cremation became the preferred method by 50.2 percent of families, edging up from 48.5 percent in 2015.

In an anything-goes age, it's useful to listen to our brothers and sisters in the Roman Catholic Church on the subject of what to do with cremated remains. In the fall of 2016, the Vatican decreed that ashes should be preserved in cemeteries or other approved sacred places. Thus, ashes should not be kept in the home, transformed into diamonds or coral reefs, blasted into outer space, scattered at sea, etc.

Explaining the Roman Catholic church position, Cardinal Gerard Ludwig Muller pointed out that the church believes in the resurrection of the body, and in that spirit cannot accept "erroneous ideas about death, such as considering death as the definitive annihilation of the person, or the moment of fusion with Mother Nature or the universe, or as a stage in the cycle of regeneration, or as the definitive liberation from the 'prison' of the body."

An author of this book and his spouse have reserved space for two sets of ashes in the columbarium of their church. It's on a busy street just off the campus of a major university—a lively environment.

Funeral home considerations

The local funeral home first became an important part of every community in years following the Civil War. Burial in the ground in a cemetery was understood as the proper disposition of the body. That's no longer true, as the majority preference for cremation indicates.

Funeral homes have adapted. Cremation often is performed at the funeral home itself. Many funeral homes welcome and are experienced at contracting for services in advance, such as arranging to transport the body from the place of death to the funeral home, holding the body intact for a day or two while survivors can assemble and have a viewing, and then cremating the remains. It's common for advance payments for the services of a funeral home to be held in trust by an insurance company.

And if there are no plans for death, which is still true in most cases, the local funeral home immediately comes to mind as the best place for survivors to make arrangements.

Cremation services

Cremation services are widely available, as an online search will reveal. Some, like Neptune Society, offer a prepaid package of services including removal of the body from the place of death, preparation of death certificates and obituary, individual cremation, and presentation of the ashes to family.

Life forever in cyberspace, or not

Finally, there's this matter of your fascinating presence on Facebook. Not long after the news of your death has circulated in phone calls among loved ones, it will almost certainly be recognized more widely through social media. Your planning should include a conversation with a close friend or family member who is adept at managing social media, with specific instructions about what you want done with the "You" in all those ethereal places such as Facebook, Twitter, and LinkedIn. Passwords to your various accounts are essential, so be sure to pass them along to your cyberspace manager.

If your advocate has the password, for example, to your Facebook account, the account can be deleted, if that's your decision. Lacking the password but with a death certificate (added to the list earlier in this chapter) and with proof of the relationship to the deceased, the advocate can ask Facebook to delete the account. Facebook also offers the option at "If I

Die" for you to create a video or text message to be published after you die, upon verification of death. If this sounds interesting, be sure to talk it over with family and friends.

For reflection:

O God, our Creator, you called us into this fragile life, assist us to recognize this reality so that we can carefully guide those who will carry on at the day of our death, through Him who died and rose for us.

CHAPTER 6

The Funeral Service

- **"Characterized by joy"**
- **Caskets**
- **Eulogies**
- **Flowers**

If planning your funeral service feels like the penultimate ego trip, and you don't really want to go there, think about it this way: it's not about you. It's about your family and friends and your whole community, the once-a-lifetime opportunity for all these other people to come together and acknowledge in heart and voice how grateful they are that you have been part of their lives. Especially when immediate family live at some distance, the gathering for your funeral connects them, often for the first time, with the many other people who have figured in your life and defined in many ways the person you became. (Indeed, family may be surprised by who shows up!)

If your circle of friends and acquaintances is small, your death will create a huge void in their lives, too. And if you discuss advance plans with your circle, you'll be saying that you care about them deeply (even though some may think at the time that it's more an amusement). So, are funerals important? Absolutely.

The sit-down talk with family: early planning

Your funeral plans will begin with a conversation with family members. Rest easy: funerals are familiar; we've all attended them. Funerals are orderly, predictable, reassuring. And because the event is some years in the future, your agenda can be bold strokes—big decisions like whether you want a service in a church or a funeral home, whether your decision is for cremation or cemetery burial, thoughts about a reception after the service and where that might be held, thoughts about who might be invited to speak a eulogy, thoughts about where immediate family and close friends live and how long it will take them to come home. The choice of a Saturday service held 10 to 14 days after death may make travel easier for some folks.

You can discuss whether there should be a reception after the service, and if so where it should be held and who would most likely make the arrangements—probably not a family member, who will be consumed with other things; better a person at the reception site.

The sit-down chat with your pastor

We're calling it a "chat" because this is just an early, informal connection with a person who perhaps will preside at your funeral, though that's not a certainty: many clergy have relatively short tenure compared to the person who has died, simply because of a difference in age or changes among church staff. But if your church office encourages members to prepare a form expressing decisions on funeral details—and you've prepared and filed such a form—you have an agenda for the chat.

(If you're unfamiliar with the kind of form referenced, you can find examples online. One is at the website of Christ Lutheran Church, in York, PA: christlutheranyork.com, "Funeral Planning Worksheet".)

A good early chat will widen your understanding of what the funeral service means in your community of faith, and will help your religious leader to make some broad decisions with you about the lessons that will be shared and the hymns that will be sung, assuring that the service will in every way possible reflect the life of faith that you have led. You may want to confirm that there will be prayer books and hymnals for everyone attending, or a printed program covering everything, including spoken responses by the congregation. The full participation of the people attending your funeral becomes vibrant testimony to what your life has meant to them.

If it's unlikely you'll be able to speak directly with a minister or priest about your funeral plans, you can quickly find the general funeral rites for your faith in an online search, for example, "United Methodist Church Funeral." In the Episcopal Church, *The Book of Common Prayer* presents the eight steps of a complete burial rite for Episcopalians, and it's easily adapted. To see the eight steps: bcponline.org/PastoralOffices/burialorder.

Sometimes the officiant at an Episcopal "Order for Burial" will read aloud this note in the prayer book:

"The liturgy for the dead is an Easter liturgy...characterized by joy, in the certainty that 'neither death, nor life, nor principalities, nor things present, nor things to come, nor powers, nor height, nor depth, nor anything else in all creation, will be able to separate us from the love of God in Christ Jesus our Lord.

"This joy, however, does not make human grief unchristian. The very love we have for each other in Christ brings deep sorrow when we are parted by death. Jesus, himself, wept at the grave of his friend. So, while we rejoice that one we love has entered into the nearer presence of our Lord, we sorrow in sympathy with those who mourn."

Compensation of church staff

The people who conduct your funeral in a church setting are the pastor or priest, other vested helpers such as acolytes, the organist or pianist, the soloists or choir, and the producer of printed material such as a service program. Not to mention the volunteer family member who has mobilized all these people for your funeral! Have you thought about who that family member or close friend will be—and asked if she or he is willing? Yes, it's years in the future but an important item to think about now.

Your chat with the clergy person should include some discussion of customary compensation of everyone who has a role in your funeral. In general, people who provide music will be paid, as will people who directly assist the religious leader in conducting the rites, such as servers in a service of holy communion, if that's part of the service. Compensation of the religious leader varies. Some clergy consider funerals part of their overall leadership role, for which they're already compensated. Others may accept a payment from family to help fund the general mission of the church. Your best advice on these money matters will come from either the religious leader you chat with early-on or the church office, or both. And be sure to pass along to the family member who will be in charge of funeral matters everything you've learned.

Service in a funeral home

The important to-do in advance of a service in a funeral home is to arrange for a printed program containing all the lessons, psalms, prayers, and songs that will be used in the service, so that everyone attending can participate and take the program home as a permanent reminder of your life. The funeral home can print the program if it receives a draft in advance; or the family can assemble and print the program. Your job is to think about what you'd like attendees to hear and see and add their voices to at the service. The person who will preside at the service and the funeral home staff can help you with the selection of readings and songs.

And speaking of songs, you may think of some that have special meaning to you that are not often heard in funeral gatherings, like the reader of *The New York Times* seeking advice from the "Social Qs" columnist. He asked whether it would be okay to include in his dad's funeral the song that he and Dad had laughed about over the years, "Papa Was a Rolling Stone". He was advised to defer to his mother, who was "violently opposed" to including a pop song in the funeral service, and to think of the song more as "a vivid memory of time with your dad" than as a melody that would be meaningful to others attending the funeral who perhaps knew him less well.

Caskets

Years ago, it was routine to place the body of a recently deceased person in an open casket so that the community could verify—see for themselves—that the person had died. You can imagine how, otherwise, a closed casket might have been used by an unscrupulous person to concoct a "death" for nefarious purposes. Today, a death is recorded by a death certificate issued by an attending physician or a coroner who has seen the body and confirmed identity. So a closed casket is okay though routinely it's open for viewing, particularly when it takes some time for family and close friends to arrive for the funeral.

Be sure to talk about the kind of casket you prefer when you discuss with family. And think about what happens to the casket after services. In the case of cremation, the casket is consumed in flames, explaining why the choice may be a simple wooden or paperboard casket. With cemetery burial, after services are over the casket is forever out of sight, placed either in a stone mausoleum above ground or lowered into a concrete vault at the gravesite and covered with earth. Over time, the body will deteriorate no matter how fancy the casket, so neither casket nor vault need be hermetically sealed.

For further perspective, think about the funeral you attended in a church where you saw the casket covered top and sides by a large cloth, something like a blanket. It's called a *pall,* from the Latin *pallium,* "covering or cloak." The word is most commonly used today in a phrase like "casting a pall," meaning spreading gloom. But in a religious setting, the purpose of a pall is simply to treat everyone the same, irrespective of the fanciness of the casket that the pall is covering. Having a very elaborate and expensive casket may be unnecessary in a church setting, and possibly elsewhere during the funeral.

Eulogies

Eulogies are becoming a regular part of funeral gatherings, and it's good planning to think about whom you'd like to sing your praises and where those tributes should be expressed. So, do run some ideas past family and friends at your next conversation.

The familiar settings for a eulogy are the religious service or the reception—or both. If the funeral is a worship service in a faith community, a eulogy is often permissible but not necessary. The formal language of the religious rite expresses what's in everyone's heart, the promise of eternal life; and the sermon by the religious leader connects the person's life with faith in a scriptural setting. But that's not a eulogy, which is a reflection by a family member or friend who has known the person for many years. If that's what you'd like as part of the religious service, be sure to talk about it in your planning chat with the religious leader. It's best in a religious setting to have just one person offer a eulogy. And as you think about the person you'd like to ask to speak for you, consider how able that person will be to retain his or her composure in a most difficult emotional setting.

The reception is in many ways a better setting for eulogies. Remembering you with laughter and tears is a huge emotional relief for everyone. If several people will be offering remembrances and tributes to you, it's best to appoint someone as emcee just to keep things moving along. A very good eulogy can be spoken in less than five minutes.

Flowers

Flowers are a beautiful gift to a family mourning a loss.

Flowers are also a management problem after the church service is over or the last person leaves the reception. What to do with the flowers left behind?? Too often, lovely bunches go into the trash.

It's time for a new flower management strategy: enlist the people who arrange flowers at the funeral service, the cemetery, or the reception to make it easy for attendees to take the flowers home with them when the services are over. And let everyone know that's okay. Yes, it's possible to manage the flower "problem" with an obit notice "...in lieu of flowers..." but some will probably arrive anyway, and the suggestions here will help others to enjoy the blossoms for days after the services.

Graveside

If the plan is for burial of the casket in the ground or placing in a mausoleum, discuss with family the importance of someone witnessing that the job is finished. That may sound obvious—completing the interment. But for incidental reasons, families sometimes are discouraged by cemetery workers or funeral directors from staying to observe that the grave is closed or the casket rolled into its place in the stone wall. Lunch breaks do interrupt cemetery work—perfectly understandable. But sometimes workers postpone and forget, and caskets are not completely placed, as they should be. It's okay for the family to ask to stay at graveside and help with shovels, or by the mausoleum to see that all is finished. Some officiating clergy will stay to witness lowering of the casket into the vault and covered with dirt, so they can later report to family that interment is complete.

For reflection:

Almighty God, who pours out on all who desire it the spirit of grace, send your Holy Spirit to guide our deliberations in preparing the worship for the celebratory gathering of friends and loved ones at our funeral.

(Adapted from *The Book of Common Prayer*)

CHAPTER 7

Downsizing

- Clothing, books, furniture
- Cats and dogs
- Cars
- Money
- Getting help to manage your downsizing
- Keeping perspective on downsizing

You may have heard this, but just so you understand from the top: the younger generation have little interest in receiving most of those treasures that surround you in your household. Your overstuffed leather sofa, the dining table with hand-carved legs, the immaculate silver service for 16, the Royal Doulton figurines, the Lenox dinnerware, the encyclopedia on the worktable, the worktable.

Don't take it personally. Many people under 40—millennials by name—live in a different world. While older folks find comfort in acquiring "household goods," and inviting company to sit in the Eames chair by name or the Barcelona, the younger generation are more interested in acquiring experiences and making connections, and neither of those interests has anything to do with household furnishings. They love you deeply; they just don't want your stuff. That doesn't mean you should leave them out of your thinking: your downsizing plans should be on the agenda for conversation.

And, of course, there are one or two things in your place that younger family members have admired and said, "Grandma, don't ever give that away—I want it." So, a tag goes somewhere on the side or back, reserved. And it's your right as the senior member to earmark other things, tokens of family history, small things to pass along, like Great-Grandma's wedding band, Grandpa's cowboy hat—keepsakes, symbols of love more than anything.

Clearing the closet

Millennials aside, most neighborhoods have surprisingly large numbers of places that will be interested in receiving a donation of your—let's start with your clothing, those closets jammed with favorite outfits from a few years ago. Sorting through a closet should be easy, but it's not. You probably will remember exactly where and when you bought (or received the gift of) almost everything on the hangers.

Women's clothing and accessories are far more interesting than men's and have better prospects for passing along or selling. For example, designer shoes and handbags, and ladieswear with fancy labels, can fetch surprising dollars in consignment shops. An online search "Consignment shops near me" will probably show a few places where you can deal. Ebay is another option, of course. And don't forget: You don't have to manage this whole sorting-out process yourself. Ask around among friends to see if you can find a younger person to become your hired hand. A millennial perhaps?

It should be easy to pass along clean, decent clothing for reuse in your community. Goodwill, The Salvation Army, and Dress for Success come to mind. If you're stumped about where to donate, call your church office. Many churches routinely collect clothing to route to local residents in need.

Books

Unless you have first editions by well-known authors, or ancient tomes that should be under glass in a museum, most of your books probably have little value in the marketplace. You can run a check on the ones you think are exceptional at the website AbeBooks. You may see other people offering the same book for sale.

Some public libraries welcome gifts of books of any vintage, not to add to their collections but to stock the library bookstore with titles offered for sale cheap, which includes books pulled from the library's own shelves because they're no longer useful to readers. If charitable deductions from income tax still interest you, ask for a receipt for your donation. You'll have to decide the dollar value, and it's probably not more than a few dollars. Other local organizations welcome books for occasional fundraisers—you may have heard their seasonal requests for donations, so it should not be hard to clear your shelves of books. You can pay a teenager to tote them off.

Of course, you'll keep some books forever because the owner signature inside the front cover is precious, or the binding is tattered in an interesting way.

Cats and dogs

Your pet cat or dog (or both if you live in mixed company) is, among many other things, the most prized possession in your household. (Residents of Seattle and San Francisco understand this well. In both cities, household dogs outnumber children.) You love your pet, and vice versa. That makes it hard to think about life apart, and hard to make plans for another home for your cat or dog.

But if it's just impossible for you to keep your pet and you want to find a good, new home, finding the best placement could begin by talking it over with a family member or friend. If your immediate group of advisors can't themselves provide the new home, they may be able to provide connections to reliable prospects. For guidance about rehoming a dog or cat, look at the website bestfriends.org. And note well the warnings about commercial pet dealers.

If your pet succumbs to accident or illness, a veterinarian can arrange for cremation and delivery of ashes to you. Some funeral homes also offer pet cremation services.

But if you should die before your pet and you want to remain physically close to the animal in the afterlife, another option that's possible in some places is to have the cremated remains of the pet buried next to you in the cemetery where you've been laid to rest. You'll need to check with local cemetery regulations to confirm if this is an option. And talk it over with family and friends.

Cars

Donating your car or other vehicle to a local nonprofit organization can be an excellent way to support community public services. Four examples of such services: PBS television; NPR radio; the National Council Society of St. Vincent de Paul; Goodwill. There are others, but these are widely known.

Generally, you assign your title to the vehicle to the organization, which arranges to take the vehicle away and sell it to a third-party buyer. The proceeds go to the nonprofit organization and you receive credit for a charitable donation to use as a tax deduction, if you wish. If you or a friend can drive the vehicle directly to the receiving organization, so much the better. That saves the recipient the cost of paying for pick-up.

The Society of St. Vincent de Paul accepts in addition to cars, donations of trucks, motorcycles, trailers, and boats. The contact number is 800-322-8284. The Society describes its work as providing "developmental programs, food, water, and shelter to those in need."

Besides the widely-known nonprofit organizations named above, some for-profit companies also seek car donations to support charitable work. But to get the most good work done with your donation, it's best to donate directly to a non-profit organization, which will have a 501(c)(3) public charity status.

Furniture (Help!)

Obviously, the largest and most difficult household items are the tables, chairs, hutches, bookcases, entertainment centers, china cabinets, sideboards, beds. Have we missed anything? The patio furniture? Stuff in the basement and garage? Because you're a well-organized type, you've already figured out what will fit into your new home and tagged everything that will move with you. And that leaves—room for professional advice, perhaps?

Downsizing Services

If sorting through all the household furnishings is more than you care to handle right now, you may want to retain the services of a specialist. The National Association of Senior Move Managers, a Chicago-area company, can put you in touch with someone at the website nasmm.com and the subheading "Find a Senior Move Manager," where you enter your zip code. It's routine to get an estimate of charges before engaging a service. Hourly rates are in the $50 to $125 range, according to the association. A move manager will have to spend some time with you, helping you sort through your possessions and identifying what will move to your new space, what should go into an estate sale, what to donate, what to trash, and even arranging for the move, if you want.

Auctioning household items online is another possibility, and local auctioneers can be helpful. Check online for auctioneers near you. One company in that business is the Cincinnati firm EBTH, which stands for "Everything But The House". Information at the website says they'll send a staffer to your home to identify sellable items, describe and photograph each item, give you an inventory, and remove the sellable things from the home. The auction posting at EBTH.com remains in place for seven days, all bids starting at $1. The company also manages payment to you and delivery to the buyer. Consultation at your home is free, and the company arranges for donations or for trash removal of things that have little or no further value.

"Antiques Roadshow"

This hugely popular PBS program is fun to watch, if only to see the enormous variety of items people tote in from attics, closets, living rooms, barns, basements, safe-deposit boxes, etc. The Monday-night TV show is always entertaining, and you may see an antique that's just like one you'd like to—keep? sell? donate to a good cause?

"Antiques Roadshow" also illustrates human nature. If you're familiar with the program, you know that each little segment ends with a declaration by the "expert" of the "market value" of the item that the person has brought in. That's when you see in the owner's face—surprise? delight? disappointment? dashed hopes? When you're downsizing, it's worth remembering that "market value" says nothing about so many household treasures, things you'll love to pass along simply because they are priceless.

Old linens, towels

Call your local animal shelter. Many are happy to receive old towels, sheets, linens, even t-shirts. Shelters use these donations to line pet cages and make warm bedding, to dry wet dogs and clean up messes.

Items in storage

Say it isn't so—you have an off-site storage locker, too?! The authors' advice is to not go there yourself but to hire someone you know and trust, like a teenage grandchild, to inventory what's in storage, report back to you for decisions about what to keep or throw, and to sell or give away give away all the rest.

Money

Your conversations with the younger generation have included money, haven't they? The family now have a pretty good understanding of where your money comes from, what your bills amount to, where you keep savings and investments, your insurance policies, where to find your financial advisor or accountant if you have one. You've also provided the name of the person who has power of attorney to manage your finances if you become unable to do so.

Looking at the much brighter side, if you have money to pass along, consider doing so now, while you're still in great shape. The recipients probably can use the money now, and you can receive their thanks in person. But note that unless you're a tax expert, you'll probably want to hire professional advice before you begin distributing your wealth. There are annual limits on cash gifts that trigger tax liabilities if exceeded. And gifts within a few years of death may be interpreted by the IRS as an attempt to avoid taxes. So, get yourself good counsel. That said, handing out your money should be a lot of fun.

Making room for a new life

For the larger picture of downsizing, consider how you can take command of your "worldly goods" with one master plan: moving to a smaller space, replacing the several thousand square feet that's been home forever for a new address that's one-third the size but just right for right now.

Moving into a smaller space removes a lot of the sting of downsizing because it provides the rationale for what you're doing: getting rid of things you've outgrown, making room for new experiences.

For reflection:

Almighty God, whose loving hand has given us all that we possess, Grant that we may honor you with our substance and remembering the accounting which we must one day give, may faithfully guide the ongoing use of our bounty.

PS: SELECTED, ANNOTATED BIBLIOGRAPHY

Following are some references that have influenced this book and may help you to reflect upon a conversation with family and other loved ones.

A Better Way of Dying: How to make the best choices at the end of life, by Jeanne Fitzpatrick, M.D.; and Eileen M. Fitzpatrick, J.D., Thorndike Press, 2010. The objective of this short (large print) book is to present an alternative to living wills and advance directives that may be more effective in preserving and applying a dying person's choices concerning health treatment at the end of life. The alternative is called "Contract for Compassionate Care," a two-page form that presents multiple-choice options for limiting medical intervention and includes the appointment of a health care decision maker. Two witnesses are required plus the signature of a physician. The contract is simple, places the emphasis on comfort care, and is designed to follow the person who prepares it. A boldface notice running across the bottom of each page says, "Send form with person whenever transferred or discharged." You can download a copy of the contract at compassionprotocol.com. It includes a short guide to considering your motives and eliminating depressive disorders from your decision to prepare the contract.

A Bittersweet Season: Caring for Our Aging Parents--and Ourselves, by Jane Gross. Vintage Books, 2011. This is not an easy read. Jane Gross, longtime reporter at *The New York Times* and founder of the blog "The New Old Age" (now moved to *nytimes.com/health*) chronicles taking care of her mother between 2000 and 2003 when "my mother's ferocious independence gave way to utter dependence on her two adult children." The book describes many of the situations that the younger, caring generation might expect as their parents grow frail and increasingly unable to take care of themselves and make decisions about their welfare. Gross shows some of the possible outcomes to even the best-planned, early conversation between generations concerning end of life. The book is especially useful as preparation for what caring people may themselves encounter. "We want to do all we realistically can to ease the suffering, smooth the passing of our loved ones," Gross writes. "But we also have the opportunity to watch what happens to our parents, listen to what they have to say to us, and use that information to look squarely at our own mortality and prepare as best we can for the end of our own lives."

"An Odyssey," by Daniel Mendelsohn. Article beginning on page 54 of April 24, 2017, *The New Yorker*. Father and son travel the route of Odysseus and conclude that the journey is what's important, not the destination.

Being Mortal: Medicine and What Matters in the End, by Atul Gawande, M.D. Metropolitan Books, 2014. This bestseller from a few years ago remains the most important book for everyone to read who has any concern about how critical life decisions are made in America today. The author, a surgeon, presents moving accounts of how patients and their families, including his own, struggle with healthcare alternatives when time grows short. From the book jacket: "Riveting, honest, and humane, *Being Mortal* shows how the ultimate goal is not a good death but a good life—all the way to the very end."

The Best Care Possible, by Ira Byock, M.D., Penguin, 2012. Some key observations: communication is the "core therapeutic medium" of palliative care; palliative care grew out of hospice care, and palliative medicine was recognized as a subspecialty in 2006; half of all men and three-quarters of all women over 75 live alone.

The Book of Common Prayer, Church Publishing Incorporated, New York, 1979. The full title adds, "and Administration of the Sacraments and Other Rites and Ceremonies of the Church, Together with The Psalter or Psalms of David, According to the use of The Episcopal Church." The preface to this book, dated "Philadelphia, October, 1789," notes its origins in the English prayer books dating to 1549-1552. Readers may find particularly useful the sections of *The Book of Common Prayer* beginning page 462, "Ministration at the Time of Death," and continuing with the language of two burial rites. The final section, on pages 506-507, titled "An Order for Burial," is a simple outline of a burial service that could be adapted for use in many situations. Unlike most other books, *The Book of Common Prayer* is not protected by copyright, a decision by the church to make it widely available. Thus, readers may copy and use any part of the book, including the texts of burial services, for example, without seeking permission from the publisher.

Caring for the Dying: The Doula Approach to a Meaningful Death, by Henry Fersko-Weiss. Conari Press, 2017. "Doula" is generally understood to mean a woman, professionally trained, who provides physical and emotional support to an expectant mother before, during, and after childbirth. This book reveals, through the eyes of an experienced professional, how a doula can bring a calming and supporting sense of order to families and caregivers at the end of life. The author and doula is Henry Fersko-Weiss, a licensed social worker, who created the first end-of-life doula program in the United States and has practiced for some years in the New York City area. His book, described as "part guidebook, part memoir," illustrates the essential non-medical services that doulas and family caregivers can provide when a loved-one nears death.

Changing the Way We Die: Compassionate End-of-Life Care and the Hospice Movement, by Fran Smith and Sheila Himmel. Viva Editions, 2014. This best-book-yet on the hospice movement chronicles the early years of hospice in America, beginning only 40 years ago, and how hospice has become today what many regard as the most successful segment of the American health-care industry.

Checklist for Family Survivors: A Guide to Practical and Legal Matters When Someone You Love Dies, by Sally Balch Hurme. American Bar Association, 2014. An exhaustive string of checklists covering just about everything of concern to family and friends when someone dies. Although the book is addressed primarily to survivors, persons planning for their own deaths will find it useful and depressing.

The Conversation: A Revolutionary Plan for End-of-Life Care, by Angelo Volandes, M.D. Bloomsbury, 2015. The often-cited sentence from Dr. Volandes's book: "Americans receive some of the best health care money can buy; they also experience some of the worst deaths in the developed world." He calls those deaths "horrible" and says they happen primarily because of "doctors' failure to discuss medical care with seriously ill patients."

The Dark Flood Rises, by Margaret Drabble, Farrar, Straus and Giroux, 2016. This 325-page novel by a celebrated British author follows the lives of a collection of Brits as they head toward the sunset, enduring pain, loneliness, expense, and indignity as the "flood" (which is death, of course) rises slowly around them. Morbid? Certainly. Depressing? One reviewer says, "Trust Margaret Drabble to take even the most worrisome of topics and make it witty, relatable and, most important, readable."

The Dead Beat, by Marilyn Johnson, Harper-Collins, 2006. Of course obituary writers have a conference! It's the Society of Professional Obituary Writers Conference, held every few years. Johnson says obit writers have a lot of fun sharing noteworthy obit phrases, like, "...a man with a subversive spirit and a body that got away from him." The *Houston Chronicle* once reported on a deceased person with the headline, "She accidentally went to Jesus." (One author of the book you're reading can report that newspaper copy editors, when they're between editions, sometimes fiddle with headlines that could be used to dispatch the famous. For Pope John Paul the Twenty-Third, the legendary example that never appeared in print, "XXIII SKIDOO.")

Digital Death: Mortality and Beyond in the Online Age. Christopher Moreman and A. David Lewis, editors. Praeger, 2014. RIP used to mean "rest in peace," suggesting a place out of touch of the living. Now it might as well mean "rest in perpetuity," thanks to the apparently eternal access living mortals have to deceased persons who have ever been enrolled in Facebook—and ignored making arrangements for their Facebook presence after death. Moreman and Lewis have put together a guide which among many other things shows survivors how to take control of the Facebook account of a person who has died. With the password, the account can be deleted, period. Lacking the password but with the death certificate and proof of relationship to the deceased, the advocate can request that Facebook delete the account. But there are other possibilities, including the Facebook application titled "If I die," described as "the digital afterlife Facebook application" that allows users "to create a video or text message that will be published after they die," upon verification of death.

Extreme Measures, by Jessica Nutik Zitter, M.D., Avery, 2017. If this book isn't in the collection at your local library, ask for it. Must-reading for everyone planning to have "the conversation" with family. Dr. Zitter draws on her experience as an ICU doc to caution against following the family exhortation to "do everything" when there is no hope of preventing death. She lists what she calls "the Big Three" kinds of emergency treatment that "Americans have come to see as their rights": breathing machines, feeding tubes, and cardiac resuscitation (CPR). "At this point in our nation's history, the Big Three are sacrosanct—if demanded they are usually delivered," she writes. And so the loved-one lies on "a conveyor belt," connected to tubes and probes, suffering the broken ribs of CPR, leading to a "mechanized death." Dr. Zitter reports a survey of 1,100 young doctors by Stanford University in 2014: nearly 90 percent said they would choose DNR—do not resuscitate—toward the end of life. The importance of this book is underscored by the people who have endorsed it on the back cover. Among others, Ira Byock, M.D.; Angelo Volandes, M.D.; and Katy Butler, all listed elsewhere in this bibliography.

The Gentle Art of Swedish Death Cleaning: How to Free Yourself and Your Family from a Lifetime of Clutter, by Margareta Magnusson, Scribner, 2018. "Death cleaning" is a Swedish expression to describe the process of clearing your household of unnecessary stuff at any time of life—but before others have to clean it for you. This charming, small book offers practical advice on getting rid of some things, saving other things, and making room for "the tiny joys that make up a long life."

The Good Death: An Exploration of Dying in America, by Ann Neumann. Beacon Press, 2016. If you expect to die a "good" death as you define it, be forewarned that your best preparation may be cast aside. "We wrongly believe that we can do what we want with our bodies, that our medical choices are our own," Neumann writes. "...We can make careful plans, we can cite when enough pain and suffering is enough, we can fill out the advance directives, the living wills, we can have the talk with our families, and still our choices can be delayed, disrupted, or completely denied." The futile "glide path" of test after test and treatment after treatment also denies these resources to other people who have a chance to live.

Good Mourning, by Elizabeth Meyer. Gallery Books, 2015. A touching, funny, irreverent, page-turner about the funeral business, a memoir by a privileged young woman who lost her father, planned his funeral, and found purpose and a new life by joining the staff of one of New York City's most celebrated funeral homes.

Good to Go: A Guide to Preparing for the End of Life, by Jo Myers. Sterling Publishing Co., 2010. From praise for this book: "If you have not yet begun to consider issues surrounding death, then you will definitely benefit from the advice in Jo Myers' book, given in a friendly, positive manner." Topics such as: the rules about scattering ashes; transporting a body across state lines; donating a body to science; access to your address book; paying for services in advance (be sure to let survivors know). About the eulogy: "The best eulogy will be written by a person who knew you well and can translate that knowledge into a succinct statement about your life and can deliver the eulogy without crying."

Greening Death: Reclaiming Burial Practices and Restoring Our Tie to the Earth, by Suzanne Kelly. 2015, Rowman & Littlefield. "It's no secret that over the last century the corpse has become increasingly hidden from sight, that the distance between the dead and the living inner circle has grown cavernous," Kelly writes. She explains how this has happened and how we can grow closer to the life of the deceased by participating in preparations for burial.

Grief Works: Stories of Life, Death and Surviving, by Julia Samuel, Penguin Life, 2017. The author is a grief psychotherapist practicing in the U.K. From the back cover: "This deeply affecting book is full of psychological insights on how grief, if approached correctly, can heal us…we learn how we can stop feeling awkward and uncertain about death, and not shy away from talking honestly with family and friends." Samuel recounts her conversations over an extended period with people who have lost partners, siblings, parents, children. In the chapter titled "Facing your own death" we listen in as Samuel counsels Jean, Barbara, and Gordon, three people nearing the end of life.

How to Get the Death You Want: A Practical and Moral Guide, by John Abraham. Upper Access Books, 2017. The author, an Episcopal priest, advocates the right to die. He works with an organization called Final Exit Network, a largely volunteer group that supports people who want to learn about hastening death; but the organization does not provide any means or assistance with accomplishing death. Abraham provides useful guidance about "advance directives"—the documents and documented understandings that provide some assurance that your wishes concerning health care toward the end of life will be respected, such things as "Durable Health Care Power of Attorney", "Physician Orders for Life-Sustaining Treatment (POLST), "Living Will". In an appendix to the book the author presents his amazing collection of more than 700 "euphemisms, metaphors, and slang terms" that we use to avoid saying the D word.

How We Die, by Sherwin B. Nuland, M.D., First Vintage Books Edition, 1995. "…the definitive text on perhaps the single most universal human concern: death."

Knocking on Heaven's Door: The Path to a Better Way of Death, by Katy Butler, Scribner, 2013. A moving account of how the author (the only daughter among three siblings, thus the designated caregiver) took care of her father for four years after he suffered a stroke—he on the East Coast, she on the West Coast, with many transcontinental flights in between.

Natural Causes: An Epidemic of Wellness, the Certainty of Dying, and Killing Ourselves to Live Longer, by Barbara Ehrenreich, Hachette, 2018. This often amusing, quick read (that's available in large print) will comfort folks who have decided just to let life take its course, come what may, and annoy other Americans who like to think they're keeping destiny (spelled d-e-a-t-h) at arm's length by their intelligent decisions about lifestyle. Ehrenreich, who has a Ph.D. in cell biology, offers easy-to-skim biological proof that "we are not the sole authors of our destinies or of anything else. You may exercise diligently, eat a medically fashionable diet, and still die of a sting from an irritated bee. You may be a slim, toned paragon of wellness, and still a macrophage may decide to throw in its lot with an incipient tumor." But the author lives on. "I retain a daily regimen of stretching, some of which might qualify as yoga," she writes. "I pretty much eat what I want and indulge my vices, from butter to wine. Life is too short to forgo these pleasures and would be far too long without them."

"Losing Streak: Reflections on two seasons of loss," by Kathryn Schulz, in *The New Yorker,* Feb. 13-20, 2017, pages 66-75. A moving essay on finding meaning in loss. "No matter what goes missing, the wallet or the father, the lessons are the same," Schulz writes. "Disappearance reminds us to notice, transience to cherish, fragility to defend."

On Death and Dying, by Elisabeth Kubler-Ross, M.D., Scribner, 1969. Fifty years ago, a psychiatrist practicing in Chicago wrote a small book that examined the feelings we all share when confronted by our approaching end of life. Kubler-Ross defined five stages as we move toward death—denial, anger, bargaining, depression, acceptance. But also *release*: "It is not the end of the physical body that should worry us," she wrote. "Rather, our concern must be to live while we're alive—to release our inner selves from the spiritual death that comes while living behind a façade designed to conform to external definitions of who and what we are." Her book is widely known and quoted.

On Living, by Kerry Egan, Riverhead Books, 2016. The author is a hospice chaplain educated at Harvard Divinity School. Visiting people who have only a short time to live, Egan listens to their stories. "Promise me you'll tell my stories," an elderly woman pleads. "Maybe someone else can get wise from them." The great difference between the dying and the rest of us, Egan writes: "They know they're running out of time. They have more motivation to do the things they want to do and become the person they want to become." Nothing prevents the rest of us from "acting with the same urgency," Egan writes.

The Right to Die, by Howard Ball. Contemporary World Issues, ABC-CLIO, 2017. A current, comprehensive reference that examines the legal issues and reports the positions and arguments of the people and organizations that are identified with the right-to-die debate. From the preface: "Americans have been living much longer and, due to changes in how the medical community responds to accidents and illness, dying much more slowly and, frequently, in great pain." The book traces how "the medicalization of death" has affected the dying process. Chapter 5, "Data and Documents," presents information about how Americans die and American states' positions on assisted suicide.

Talking About Death Won't Kill You: The Essential Guide to End-of-Life Conversations, by Dr. Kathy Kortes-Miller, assistant professor, School of Social Work, Lakehead University, Thunder Bay, Ontario, Canada. ECW Press, 2018. Professor Kortes-Miller also is Palliative Care Division Lead at the Centre for Education and Research on Aging and Health at the university. One back-cover blurb: "It's hard to imagine a better guide to end-of-life conversations...I especially welcomed her consideration of the role played by social media in death and mourning." Tailored to a Canadian audience, this new book will serve Americans, too.

Walking on Eggshells: Caring for a Critically Ill Loved One, by Amy Sales, MSW. New Horizon Press, 2012. In this book, death is at the doorstep, not far distant. Chapter 11, "Caring for a Parent with a Life-Threatening Illness," offers insights into the relationship between adult children and their parents, "how their parents' status evolved from that of superheroes to mere mortals, flaws and all."

"Wit." A decade before "the medicalization of death" became the descriptor, Mike Nichols' 2001 film, "Wit," shows what it means to a dying person to endure seemingly endless tests and procedures leading to certain death. The film is an adaptation of the Pulitzer-winning stage-play of the same name. Emma Thompson plays the role of Vivian Bearing, a 48-year-old English professor diagnosed with Stage IV ovarian cancer.

"Are you sure you want to go the self-publishing route?"

INDEX

www.ingramcontent.com/pod-product-compliance
Lightning Source LLC
Chambersburg PA
CBHW050427290526
45786CB00003B/1427